This Guide has bee
into the world of

Going forward we encourage you
to pursue your own Methods,
Theology and Practices.

Every time you delve, do so with a
clear head and clearer intentions.

Trust in your gut and
Remain open minded.

"not all that glitters is gold"
Jrr Tolkien

Contents

Perth

Algiz

Sowilo

Tiwaz

Berkano

Ehwaz

Mannaz

Laguz

Ingwaz

Dagaz

Othila

What are Runes?

Runes/Picture Symbols date back to some of the earlier civilisations we know of. Often depicted in various ways they make up some of the earliest forms of the written language and have been translated by scholars for many generations. Despite the adaptions into the modern Alphabet, the potency of their original intentions can be felt throughout and are used by practitioners today to gain insight to/from the ancient world. There are many new variations of Runes with strong intentions and modern Authors like to use their likeness in novels to provide authentic settings for made up languages. While these can be seen and are available all over, this book focuses on the Elder Futhark Runes, most heavily associated with Nordic ancestry derived from Germanic Paganism. These Runes are considered/regarded as some of the oldest and most powerful amongst practitioners.

Where do they come from?

The Elder Futhark runes being some of the oldest can be traced across Europe and across other continents. Their influence has been widespread by their Pagan followers for generations. While being referred to as Germanic Pagans often associated with Germany, this is loosely accurate as their exact origin isn't known. The people of the black forest and its northern neighbours were rebellious of advancing modern religions and those labelled Pagans were considered threats to this development. This created a taboo of the word Pagan and caused such practices to be labelled blasphemy or even devil worship. But this couldn't be further from the truth as such practices have always been for the betterment of the tribes/groups and as such have been making a return in recent years. Modern culture associates these runes with Scandinavian Culture due to their references to Nordic Gods Freya, Odin and Thor etc and as such most depictions are of their heritage.

How do you Draw Runes?

Drawing/Pulling Runes can be done in many ways and looking online you can find many methods. Ultimately, we suggest that you do this in what ever way feels natural to you. We have given some suggestions, feel free to give them a go. Remember what ever results you get, go with your gut. What isn't obvious now may become clear later. Equally don't jump to conclusions, let time unfold the truth.

The Spread

A spread is the term used to refer to the order in which you pull your Runes and the questions you are asking. The most common spread used with Tarot Practitioners and Rune Readers alike is referred to as

PAST-PRESENT-FUTURE

Three Stones are drawn in this order and the results read accordingly, being direct in their request these are pulled often to give advice on general living. Some prefer answers to be more progressive from this asking

PAST-PRESENT-FUTURE-AIDS-HINDRANCES

The follow up looks for what can help with a situation and what could cause issues along the way.

Pulling the Runes

How to draw Runes is also considered
personal so choose your own method,
but here is a couple of suggestions.

Open your Runes Satchel, close your eyes and
focus on your question. While doing this take in a
long breath then exhale into the Satchel blowing
the question from your mind into the bag.
Once you have done this, blindly pull the stones
in the order of your chosen spread. As they are
advice you may wish to consider which way the
stones are facing when pulled, many believe that
there can be inverted interpretations often giving
warnings or "tellings off" we have included these.
Another method is having a cloth down,
empty the Rune bag, close your eyes and lift
the stones intuitively this is a popular method
feeling authentic to many. Again consider
your question and how you lift the Runes
as inverted messages maybe waiting.

Disclaimer

As we have said what you do with the information provided and how you interpret the Runes is deeply personal and must always be done with a level of caution. Only the etchings are set in stone, the meanings are as fluid as life itself.

We hope you find enlightenment from this practice and are guided to good fortune

Now begin your journey

Fehu

(Fey-hoo)

Associated with the Goddess Freya

Translates as Cattle and Wealth

Fehu often refers to prosperity through physical gain. Owning cattle was (and is) considered a strong asset as it provides sustenance and fortune to its owner. This can be interpreted as the possibility of receiving a fiscal gain in the near future. This can also be a hint to take stock and be thankful for the prosperity that you have, wealth comes in many forms and you should not ignore this. The Cow being a loving creature symbolises the birth of new relationships and new beginnings so embracing a romantic gesture should be considered.

<u>Inversed</u>

An inverted Fehu refers to being guarded and protecting your assets. In love a break-up could be on the horizon if caution is not taken.

Uruz

(oo-rooz)

Translated as Oxen

Uruz is a Rune of brute strength, referring to an ancient form of bull known for its long horns (like the rune depicts) and volatile temperament. This rune often suggest that we need strength at this time and must embrace our animal instinct to charge forward into a situation, courage and bravado are key here. Good strong health is depicted and seeks to continue. This does however also warn against bull headedness towards some situations as opportunities may pass you by.

Inversed

Inversed this rune suggests that you have allowed your anger or determination to get ahead of you and need to take stock of the situation. Guard your health in this moment as illness could strike

Thurisaz

(thur-ree-saz)

Associated with the God Thor

Translates as Thor or Thorn

This is considered a Rune of protection, guarding against forces known or considered. The rune, shaped as a thorn suggests entering situations with protection as threats are near. Approach this rune and situations as you would a rose, what appears beautiful and delicate has hidden defences. A wrong move could end in folly.

Inversed

Inversed this Rune suggests not approaching guarded, perhaps defensive stance could lead to further issues. Look at the situation prevented and consider the possibility that being less guarded could yield better results.

Ansuz

(an-sooz)

Translates as Ancestral God

This Rune gives guidance to open up lines of communication. This maybe a communion with those around you and an opportunity to open up about things you have kept close. This is considered a good omen around interviews and talking situations. It can also suggest to open a line of communication with celestial beings, your higher self, ancestors and deities as they are seeking to give advice.

<u>Inversed</u>

This is a time to be guarded, giving out information or to much information could be dangerous. There is deceit and trickery at play. Weigh everyword carefully and view situations carefully before acting.

Raido

(ri-tho)

Translates as wagon or riding

Being the Rune of travel this often suggests an imminent journey, however this can be physical, metaphysical or emotional. This is a positive omen for any journey as it guide us to the sense that we are going in the right direction and that any disturbances are/will be minor if any. If there something you have been putting off, now seems the time to act.

<u>Inversed</u>

Inversed this Rune suggest that a journey is not going well, or likely to hit problems. While it does not specify an end to a journey, caution must always be taken and protection considered.

Kenaz

(kay-naz)

Translates as fire or beacon

A beacon of hope and warmth in your life this Rune signifies a source of enlightenment or illumination of a situation. You are able to see clearly that which was kept dark and are internally warmed by this information or revelation.

Inversed

Inversed is the lose of this light, your are feeling cold hidden and in the dark. You must seek the light and warmth, making no effort to do so will keep you in the dark.

Gebo

(gay-bo)

Translates as Gift or Generosity

While physical gifts are pleasant, this is often more associated with gifts of friendship, trust and even love. Embrace and accept gratefully the gifts of others as they strive to give to you. This Rune is symmetrical and mirrors that idea that any gift received must be repaid in kindness, in relationships that can be signal that a dept of gratitude is to be paid and should not be ignored

Wunjo

(woon-yo)

Translates as Joy or Hope

The is a rune of Positivity and in certain spreads when being asked a question, this is a positive Yes. Considered a hand on your shoulder Wunjo is the gift of hope from higher up that a situation will get better and positive thinking is key to achieving this. Relationships are feeling a positive turn if there has been tension.

Inversed

You could be in the middle of a tense time emotionally and physically. The strength to continue is wavering, you must not give in to this as it will continue. Relationships are at their most strained but positivity even in this tough time is needed.

Hagalaz

(haga-laz)

Translates as Hailstone

Considered to be the destructive forces of Nature this Rune remind us that there are things out with our control. You may be witnessing or on the brink of a situation that makes you feel helpless, this may be the case. But this is your moment to step back, find shelter and let what will be, be. Don't feel useless, no one can hold back the storm, we must all ride it out. Remember that bad weather is often followed by a rainbow.

Nauthiz

(now-theez)

Translate as Need

It's time to look at yourself and decide what
is needed, this Rune shows it's self when
someone's needs aren't being met. It could be
emotional, physical, fiscal, psychological or any
variant of this. The point is, take a moment and
decided what needs to happen to help whoever
needs it right now. In relationships you or
your partner wants contact and embracing
this will help you both move forward

Isa

(ee-saa)

Translated as Ice

Isa represents the great obstacles that life throws at us. The crushing strength of Ice should never be underestimated and sometimes no matter how much we hack at the wall, we only chip away at the problem. Look for another angle, should you walk around the obstacle or show patience. When the Sun shines Ice eventually melts and so do life's problems.

Jera

(year-a)

Translates as Harvest

You have worked hard and the fruits of your labour are coming to bare, but more hard work is still needed. Just as grain does not harvest its self, now is not the moment to rest on your laurels. A good harvest can be spoiled if not worked at the correct time so take care to make sure that everything is where it is meant to be. Also remember that a farmer does not stop once the harvest has finished, preparations must be made to sow for the future.

Eithwaz

(ey-whaz)

Translates as Yew

This rune bears similarity to the Death card in Tarot. Those who don't know, see death as an omen of evil. But in divination this is the symbol of rebirth, with the death of one begins the birth of another. This is an opportunity to start a fresh and take new perspective, don't mourn an ending but rejoice a beginning.

Perth/Pertho

(per-tho)

Translation is unclear

Just as the translation is mystery, this rune symbolises secrets and possibly deception.

If you are keeping a secret or trying to discover a secret, it is clear that a mental guard is required right now to discover the truth. Don't go head long into anything as not all is as it appears and haste may prove folly in discovering the truth.

Inversed

While unclear if this symbol can be inversed, many consider it to be the concealment of a dark truth to be wary of. Sometimes we find out things we dont want to and while all truths will out, now may not be the right time.

Algiz

(al hiz)

Translates as Protection

Being akin to Pitch forks in many cultures and antlers in others, this is a rune of protection and divine strength. It represents your guarded stance holding a weapon of power and protection at this time, but warns that being confident is different to being ready for an attack so take care. In some cases this image represents man reaching up and requesting a connection with divine forces whether for protection or guidance.

Inversed

Drawn inversed this a rune of warning that you have let your guard down and are currently unprotected, therefore must take steps immediately. There are perhaps messages you have missed or misinterpreted and should seek further guidance.

Sowilo

(so-weelow)

Translates as Sun

A great light like no other, the Sun rune is a representation of all things warm and light. It allows all life to bask in its presence, feel its blanket upon your shoulders, know that this is a time to open up and feel free for the darkness (for now) has been banished. You might have been feeling in the dark for sometime but now must take this opportunity to enjoy the fruits of the day, darkness will always return but you must seize this moment.

Tiwaz

(tee-waz)

Translates as the God Tyr

In the tales of old, Tyr was a great God. Even considered a protector of Gods having sacrificed his hand to protect Odin from Fenrir the great wolf. This Rune is a homage to sacrifice for victory and tells us that we need courage in this time. You might be faced with a dilemma that you know will cost you, ultimately the sacrifice though potentially painful will be for the best and you will be remembered heroically for it. Tyr is considered the strength of man and urges you as a male so seek courage within or as a female to embrace the protection of a man in your life.

Inversed

Being a rune of great courage, inversed is sadly telling you that you are currently lacking in this quality and need to address why. Perhaps the challenge ahead is difficult but you need to consider the consequences and/or those who might be hurt if you don't find a way forward.

Berkano

(ber-can-o)

Translates as Birch

Rejoice in the time of new beginnings, this Rune is a omen of all things new and wonderful to enter the world. Berkano represents the mother of all, Earth and the strength of women to be embraced. The protection of the great mother is a place of warmth and comfort allowing all things to grow and mature. Taken literally this rune gives a positive omen around childbirth. A more metaphysical meaning, it can mean simply the change or rebirth of an individual, either way it is a time of great happiness and should be enjoyed by all.

<u>Inversed</u>

No jumping to conclusions, but some do see this as an omen of problems around a birth. Not necessarily life threatening but care should be taken at this time. In a broader translation it can be seen as a moment of stagnation and little change, you are in the cocoon but nothing is happening and must do something to change this.

Ehwaz

ᛗ

(eh-waz)

Translates as Horse

In the times of old, the horse was revered as a powerful, loyal and dependable companion to its keeper and this bond is represented by this rune. Ehwaz is a rune of strong relationships formed through trust and experience. It tells us to lean on those we count on the most, that they will bare our weight and help us move forward so long as we remember to return the same care and loyalty.

<u>Inversed</u>

You or someone you care about is not showing
the loyalty or commitment require for a healthy
relationship and this must be addressed or one/
both of you will seek greener pastures elsewhere.

Mannaz

(ma-naz)

Translates as Mankind/Human

Mannaz is a strange rune as it depicts the separation between man and beast. While nature carries on its timeless dance, Man seeks to create, build and deeply consider their place in the wide universe beyond simply staying alive. In a positive light this rune encourages inner and outer development, it asks us to look within and embrace the qualities that make us unique as an individual. Take a moment to develop a quality that you poses and move forward

<u>Inversed</u>

You seem to be in a physical and/or mental rut
and it is stopping you from living your best life.
Take this moment to reflect upon this, the symbol
for Mannaz is a structure and sometimes only
needs one missing piece to give it the strength
to hold firm allowing you to move forward.

Laguz

(la-gooz)

Translates as Water

Laguz much like a swift river is a torrent of possibility and potential dangers to be tackled. Water as an element represents the flow of all energy, always finding its way in and out through the smallest imperceivable ways. It allows us to heal and can cause us great pain when taken for granted, therefore should never be underestimated. Experience and intuition are the guidance here, much like a river you are recommended to go with the flow however, knowing where the rapids are on the river is important. You should pull your boat out of the water and find a new route when threatened.

<u>Inversed</u>

This is a warning that you have been neglecting your intuition or ignoring experience, the river is rough ahead and will come to folly without swift action. Just because the water looks calm now does not mean there is not danger, a small stream now always leads to open water.

Ingwaz

(ing-waz)

Translates as the God Ing

Ingwaz is a binding of family protection, often seen as male fertility it is the protection a father figure gives to his family. As the fathers role in creation ends, a new beginning is on the horizon signalling great change for the individuals involved. Taken literally this could point towards a new family member on the way, in more loose terms this rune is about the changes someone undergoes to embrace new challenges ahead. Just as a man becomes a father and should embrace the role to protect and provide, you must accept and embrace your new path and give your best effort to protect those you care for.

Dagaz

(dah-gaz)

Translates as Day

Dagaz represents the dawning of a new day. As Sowillo banishes the dark and dangerous, Dagaz is the balance held, that it is simply daylights turn to shine before the night returns. You must understand the balance of all things, that there cannot be light without the dark and choosing to embrace those moments is the key to moving forward. Sure the night will set in and in different seasons this lasts longer than others, but the light will always come back. Never loose faith that even when things seem dark now, when you wake up in the light there is endless opportunities to be grasped.

Othila

(o-thi-la)

Translates as Inheritance
Associated with God Odin

Othila the final rune, is the rune of family. As we are all children of the all father, this rune represents the ties and bonds of family stretching back through generations. Pulling this rune is considered the to be a tap on the shoulder from our ancestors to let us know that they are watching and wish to help or guide us where they can. There is great wealth not in the soil of earth but in the strength of family and remembering our past can help us towards the future. This rune tells us to seek the strength of our family whether near, distant or ethereal you must reach out and embrace their help.

<u>Inversed</u>

Your family is currently in a moment of strife
and either you or they needs to put petty
differences aside to remember the bonds of blood.
Continue to seek resolve and consider lessons
of the past when you seek familiar embrace.

We hope you have enjoyed this book and will continue your study. The translations and meanings we have given are open to everyone's interpretation and reading elsewhere will show you, further, deeper and more elaborate interpretations that will guide you further.

If you don't have a rune set yet
check out our website
www.hatterskreations.com
to purchase your first set and begin
your divination journey.

Printed in Great Britain
by Amazon